T0040309

Contents

Introduction

There are a few auspicious days that define a person's life, and graduation is one of them. It doesn't matter whether you're completing middle school, high school, college, or grad school, as soon as you put on those hot, uncomfortable robes and that stupid-looking hat, you are on the cusp of a boundary dividing "before" and "after," the end of an era and the start of a new one.

Sure, this is an exciting time for anyone, but let's be honest: graduation can also be utterly terrifying. One day, you're a callow youth with hardly a care in the world; the next, you are—for lack of a better word—a grownup, venturing into the Great Unknown of Adulthood. That's definitely a scary thought, but this transition means more than simply leaving childhood behind.

Graduation is the first step to truly living. It is the moment when you accept your responsibilities as an adult and are expected to fulfill some sort of role in society, and while those are some awfully tall orders, graduation is also the first time you are able to do what you want with your life, without anyone holding you back or telling you no. The world is a big, beautiful (and yes, sometimes scary) place, and the only way to experience it is to live as you've always wanted.

To help get you on your way, the book you hold in your hands collects quotes from the wisest minds of history and fiction—touching on everything from the different notions of success, to the responsibilities of social justice, to the best commencement speeches ever delivered. So *carpe diem*, take the road less traveled, live the life you deserve, take every shot, and—for the love of God—never, ever say "I'm bored." This, dear graduate, is your day.

Congratulations,

Michael Pipper
November 2013

1

Carpe Diem

Life moves pretty fast. If you don't stop and look around once in a
while, you could miss it.
—Ferris Bueller, *Ferris Bueller's Day Off* (1986)

• • •

Carpe diem, seize the day, boys. Make your lives extraordinary.
—John Keating, *Dead Poets Society* (1989)

• • •

Life must not be a novel that is given to us,
but one that is made by us.
—Novalis

• • •

Destiny is no matter of chance.
It is a matter of choice. It is not a thing to be waited for,
it is a thing to be achieved.
—WILLIAM JENNINGS BRYAN

• • •

Staying on the fence is safe . . . until someone shoots you off.
—STEVEN CHARLES

• • •

Follow your bliss and the universe will open doors for you where
there were only walls.
—JOSEPH CAMPBELL

• • •

If you concentrate always on the present,
you'll be a happy man.
You'll see that there is life in the desert,
that there are stars in the heavens . . . Life will be a party for you,
a grand festival, because life is the moment
we're living right now.
—PAULO COELHO, *The Alchemist* (1988)

• • •

Remembering that you are going to die is the best way I know to
avoid the trap of thinking you have something to lose.
—STEVE JOBS

• • •

Sometimes you just have to pee in the sink.
—CHARLES BUKOWSKI

• • •

Fate loves the fearless.
—JAMES RUSSELL LOWELL

• • •

Only he who attempts the absurd is capable of achieving
the impossible.
—MIGUEL DE UNAMUNO

• • •

Don't tell me I can't do it; don't tell me it can't be done!
—HOWARD HUGHES, *The Aviator* (2004)

• • •

Set your goals high, and don't stop till you get there.
—BO JACKSON

• • •

I wanna shake off the dust of this one-horse town. I wanna
explore the world. I wanna watch TV in a different time zone.
I wanna visit strange, exotic malls. I'm sick of eating hoagies.
I want a grinder, a sub, a foot-long hero.
I want to *live*, Marge.
—HOMER SIMPSON, *The Simpsons* (1994)

• • •

Life is a great big canvas; throw all the paint you can at it.
—DANNY KAYE

• • •

If there's a single lesson that life teaches us,
it's that wishing doesn't make it so.
—LEV GROSSMAN, *The Magicians* (2009)

• • •

"I'm bored" is a useless thing to say. I mean, you live in a great,
big, vast world that you've seen none percent of. Even the inside
of your own mind is endless; it goes on forever, inwardly,
do you understand? The fact that you're alive is amazing,
so you don't get to say "I'm bored."
—LOUIS C. K.

• • •

First say to yourself what you would be;
and then do what you have to do.
—EPICTETUS

• • •

Carpe Diem

Dead yesterdays and unborn tomorrows, why fret about it,
if today be sweet.
—OMAR KHAYYÁM

• • •

Grab it. Grab this land! Take it, hold it, my brothers, make it,
my brothers, shake it, squeeze it, turn it, twist it, beat it, kick it,
kiss it, whip it, stomp it, dig it, plow it, seed it, reap it, rent it,
buy it, sell it, own it, build it, multiply it, and pass it on—can
you hear me? Pass it on!
—TONI MORRISON, *Song of Solomon* (1977)

• • •

If they give you ruled paper, write the other way.
—JUAN RAMÓN JIMÉNEZ

• • •

I began to realize how important it was to be an enthusiast in life.
He taught me that if you are interested in something, no matter
what it is, go at it at full speed ahead. Embrace it with both
arms, hug it, love it, and above all become passionate about it.
Lukewarm is no good. Hot is no good either.
White hot and passionate is the only thing to be.
—ROALD DAHL, *My Uncle Oswald* (1986)

• • •

You don't win races by wishing, you win them by running faster
than everyone else does.
—PHILLIP PULLMAN, *Clockwork* (1996)

• • •

To exist in this vast universe for a speck of time is the great gift of life. Our tiny sliver of time is our gift of life. It is our only life. The universe will go on, indifferent to our brief existence, but while we are here we touch not just part of that vastness, but also the lives around us. Life is the gift each of us has been given. Each life is our own and no one else's. It is precious beyond all counting. It is the greatest value we can have. Cherish it for what it truly is. . . . Your life is yours alone. Rise up and live it.
—TERRY GOODKIND

• • •

Seize the moments of happiness, love and be loved! That is the only reality in the world, all else is folly. It is the one thing we are interested in here.
—LEO TOLSTOY, *War and Peace* (1869)

• • •

Take wrong turns. Talk to strangers. Open unmarked doors. And if you see a group of people in a field, go find out what they are doing. Do things without always knowing how they'll turn out. . . . You're curious and smart and bored, and all you see is the choice between working hard and slacking off. There are so many adventures that you miss because you're waiting to think of a plan. To find them, look for tiny interesting choices. And remember that you are always making up the future as you go.
—RANDALL MUNROE, *xkcd*

• • •

Do not dare not to dare.
—C. S. LEWIS

• • •

The world is wide, and I will not waste my life in friction when it could be turned into momentum.
—FRANCES E. WILLARD

• • •

You're *alive*, Bod. That means you have infinite potential. You can do anything, make anything, dream anything. If you can change the world, the world will change. Potential. Once you're dead, it's gone. Over. You've made what you've made, dreamed your dream, written your name. You may be buried here, you may even walk. But that potential is finished.
—SILAS, *The Graveyard Book* (2008) by Neil Gaiman

• • •

Carpe Diem

Age considers; youth ventures.
—RABINDRANATH TAGORE

• • •

I feel very adventurous. There are so many doors to be opened,
and I'm not afraid to look behind them.
—ELIZABETH TAYLOR

• • •

Action may not always bring happiness, but there is no
happiness without action.
—WILLIAM JAMES

• • •

Face front, true believer!
—STAN LEE

• • •

To live each day as though one's last, never flustered, never apathetic, never attitudinizing—here is perfection of character.
—MARCUS AURELIUS, *Meditations*

• • •

Amateurs sit and wait for inspiration, the rest of us just get up and go to work.
—STEPHEN KING, *On Writing* (2000)

• • •

Life's like a movie, write your own ending. Keep believing,
keep pretending.
—JIM HENSON

• • •

So many people walk around with a meaningless life. They seem
half-asleep, even when they're busy doing things they think are
important. This is because they're chasing the wrong things.
The way you get meaning into your life is to devote yourself to
loving others, devote yourself to your community around you,
and devote yourself to creating something that gives you purpose
and meaning.
—MITCH ALBOM, *Tuesdays with Morrie* (1997)

• • •

I believe that life is a game, that life is a cruel joke, and that life
is what happens when you're alive and that you might as well lie
back and enjoy it.
—SAM, *American Gods* (2001) by Neil Gaiman

• • •

What's comin' will come, and we'll meet it when it does.
—HAGRID, *Harry Potter and the Goblet of Fire* (2000)
by J. K. Rowling

• • •

For myself I am an optimist—it does not seem to be much use to
be anything else.
—WINSTON CHURCHILL

• • •

A ship is safe in harbor, but that's not what ships are for.
—WILLIAM G. T. SHEDD

• • •

The best way to prepare for death is to live life to its fullest.
—JOHN BYTHEWAY

• • •

I wanted change and excitement and to shoot off in all directions
myself, like the colored arrows from a Fourth of July rocket.
—SYLVIA PLATH

• • •

Faster, Faster, until the thrill of speed overcomes
the fear of death.
—HUNTER S. THOMPSON

• • •

May you live every day of your life.
—JONATHAN SWIFT

• • •

Do not let your fire go out, spark by irreplaceable spark, in the hopeless swamps of the approximate, the not-quite, the not-yet, the not-at-all. Do not let the hero in your soul perish, in lonely frustration for the life you deserved, but have never been able to reach. Check your road and the nature of your battle. The world you desired can be won, it exists, it is real, it is possible, it's yours.
—AYN RAND, *Atlas Shrugged* (1957)

• • •

Two roads diverged in a wood, and I—
I took the one less traveled by,
And that has made all the difference.
—ROBERT FROST, "The Road Less Traveled" (1920)

• • •

If we listened to our intellect we'd never have a love affair. We'd never have a friendship. We'd never go in business because we'd be cynical: "It's gonna go wrong." Or, "She's going to hurt me." Or, "I've had a couple of bad love affairs, so therefore . . ." Well, that's nonsense. You're going to miss life. You've got to jump off the cliff all the time and build your wings on the way down.
—RAY BRADBURY

• • •

You can't stay in your corner of the Forest waiting for others to come to you. You have to go to them sometimes.
—A. A. MILNE, *Winnie-the-Pooh* (1926)

• • •

Life is trouble. Only death is not. To be alive is to undo your belt and look for trouble.
—ALEXIS ZORBA, *Zorba the Greek* (1964)

• • •

Home is behind, the world ahead.
—J. R. R. TOLKIEN, *The Fellowship of the Ring* (1954)

● ● ●

To infinity, and beyond!
—BUZZ LIGHTYEAR, *Toy Story* (1995)

● ● ●

Here we are, trapped in the amber of the moment.
There is no why.
—KURT VONNEGUT

● ● ●

Life all comes down to a few moments.
This is one of them.
—BUD FOX, *Wall Street* (1987)

• • •

Get busy livin', or get busy dyin'.
—ANDY DUFRESNE, *The Shawshank Redemption* (1994)

• • •

A lot of people enjoy being dead. But they are not dead, really.
They're just backing away from life. Reach out.
Take a chance. Get hurt even. But play as well as you can.
Go team, go!
—MAUDE, *Harold & Maude* (1971)

• • •

Nothing is impossible, the word itself says "I'm possible!"
—AUDREY HEPBURN

• • •

Don't wait. The time will never be just right.
—NAPOLEON HILL

• • •

The unexamined life is not worth living.
—SOCRATES

• • •

You miss 100 percent of the shots you don't take.
—WAYNE GRETZKY

• • •

If you want to make an apple pie from scratch, you must first create the universe.
—CARL SAGAN

• • •

Twenty years from now, you will be more disappointed by the things you didn't do than by the ones you did do. So throw off the bowlines. Sail away from the safe harbor. Catch the trade winds in your sails. Explore. Dream. Discover.
—H. JACKSON BROWN, JR.

• • •

Do not go where the path may lead, go instead where there is no path and leave a trail.
—Ralph Waldo Emerson

• • •

If opportunity doesn't knock, build a door.
—Milton Berle

• • •

The only way of finding the limits of the possible is by going beyond them into the impossible.
—Arthur C. Clarke

• • •

2

Making New Friends and Keeping Old Ones

Friendship is unnecessary, like philosophy, like art . . .
It has no survival value; rather it is one of those things
that give value to survival.
—C. S. LEWIS, *The Four Loves* (1960)

• • •

Happiness is only real when shared.
—JON KRAKAUER, *Into the Wild* (1996)

• • •

Neither time nor distance can break the bonds that we feel.
—HAROLD, *The Big Chill* (1983)

• • •

No man is useless so long as he's got a friend.
—DOC VELIE, *Bad Day at Black Rock* (1955)

• • •

A friend is someone who knows all about you
and still loves you.
—ELBERT HUBBARD

• • •

It's the friends you can call up at 4 a.m. that matter
—MARLENE DIETRICH

• • •

They do not love, that do not show their love.
—WILLIAM SHAKESPEARE

● ● ●

Friendship is love without his wings.
—LORD BYRON

● ● ●

It is more shameful to distrust our friends than
to be deceived by them.
—CONFUCIUS

● ● ●

I would rather walk with a friend in the dark,
than alone in the light.
—Helen Keller

• • •

What is a friend? A single soul dwelling in two bodies.
—Aristotle

• • •

"Stay" is a charming word in a friend's vocabulary.
—Amos Bronson Alcott, *Concord Days* (1873)

• • •

Can miles truly separate you from friends . . . If you want to be
with someone you love, aren't you already there?
—RICHARD BACH

• • •

I am glad you are here with me.
Here at the end of all things, Sam.
—FRODO BAGGINS, *Return of the King* (1955) by J. R. R. Tolkien

• • •

There is nothing like puking with somebody to make
you into old friends.
—SYLVIA PLATH, *The Bell Jar* (1963)

• • •

Don't underestimate the power of friendship.
Those bonds are tight stitches that close up the holes
you might otherwise fall through.
—RICHELLE E. GOODRICH

• • •

When you're in jail, a good friend will be trying to bail you out.
A best friend will be in the cell next to you saying,
"Damn, that was fun."
—GROUCHO MARX

• • •

Cutting people out of your life is easy,
keeping them in is hard.
—WALTER DEAN MEYERS, *Slam!* (1998)

• • •

However rare true love may be,
it is less so than true friendship.
—ALBERT EINSTEIN

• • •

A friend is one who walks in when others walk out.
—WALTER WINCHELL

• • •

The bird a nest, the spider a web, man *friendship.*
—WILLIAM BLAKE, "Proverbs of Hell" (1790)

• • •

We all need to be mocked from time to time, Lord Mormont, lest
we start to take ourselves too seriously.
—TYRION LANNISTER, *A Game of Thrones* (1996)
by George R. R. Martin

• • •

We are the music-makers, And we are the dreamers of dreams,
Wandering by lone sea-breakers, And sitting by desolate streams.
World-losers and world-forsakers, Upon whom the pale moon
gleams; Yet we are the movers and shakers, Of the world forever,
it seems.
—ARTHUR O'SHAUGHNESSY, "Ode" (1874)

• • •

No man is an island, entire of itself; every man is a piece of the continent, a part of the main. If a clod be washed away by the sea, Europe is the less, as well as if a promontory were, as well as if a manor of thy friend's or of thine own were: any man's death diminishes me, because I am involved in mankind, and therefore never send to know for whom the bells tolls; it tolls for thee.
—John Donne, *Meditation XVII* (1623)

• • •

If I have the gift of prophecy and can fathom all mysteries and all knowledge, and if I have a faith that can move mountains, but do not have love, I am nothing.
—1 Cor. 13:2

• • •

Greater love has no one than this, that he lay down his life for his friends.
—John 15:13

• • •

A friend loves at all times,
and a brother is born for adversity.
—PROVERBS 17:17

• • •

I am what I am, an' I'm not ashamed. "Never be ashamed,"
my ol' dad used ter say, "there's some who'll hold it against you,
but they're not worth botherin' with."
—HAGRID, *Harry Potter and the Goblet of Fire* (2000)
by J. K. Rowling

• • •

Love, and do what you will. If you keep silence, do it out of love.
If you cry out, do it out of love. If you refrain from punishing,
do it out of love.
—AUGUSTINE OF HIPPO

• • •

It is one of the blessings of old friends that you can
afford to be stupid with them.
—Ralph Waldo Emerson

• • •

Good friends, good books, and a sleepy conscience:
this is the ideal life.
—Mark Twain

• • •

Associate yourself with people of good quality, for it is better to be alone than to be in bad company.
—BOOKER T. WASHINGTON

• • •

A trophy carries dust. Memories last forever.
—MARY LOU RETTON

• • •

Some people come into our lives and quickly go. Some stay for a while, leave footprints on our hearts, and we are never, ever the same.
—ADLAI E. STEVENSON II

• • •

3

Everything That's Important to Know

It is necessary to hope . . . for hope itself is happiness.
—Samuel Johnson

• • •

Age is a very high price to pay for maturity.
—Tom Stoppard

• • •

You can't do anything about the length of your life, but you can
do something about its width and depth.
—H. L. Mencken

• • •

Humor keeps us alive. Humor and food. Don't forget food.
You can go a week without laughing.
—Joss Whedon

• • •

One must still have chaos in oneself to be able to give birth
to a dancing star.
—Friedrich Nietzsche, *Thus Spoke Zarathustra* (1885)

• • •

Yet he who reigns within himself, and rules Passions,
desires, and fears, is more a king.
—John Milton, *Paradise Regained* (1671)

• • •

The difference between false memories and true ones is the same as for jewels: it is always the false ones that look the most real, the most brilliant.
—Salvador Dalí

• • •

The cynic is one who never sees a good quality in a man and never fails to see a bad one. He is the human owl, vigilant in darkness and blind to light, mousing for vermin, and never seeing noble game. The cynic puts all human actions into two classes—*openly* bad and *secretly* bad.
—Henry Ward Beecher, *Lectures to Young Men: On Various Important Subjects* (1844)

• • •

Never apologize for showing feeling. When you do so, you apologize for the truth.
—Benjamin Disraeli

• • •

Don't look to the approval of others for your mental stability.
—KARL LAGERFELD

• • •

You don't have to be great to get started, but you have to get
started to be great.
—LES BROWN

• • •

But it seems to me that once you begin a gesture it's fatal not to
go through with it.
—JOHN UPDIKE, "A&P" (1961)

• • •

The place to improve the world is first in one's own heart and head and hands, and then work outward from there.
—ROBERT M. PIRSIG, *Zen and the Art of Motorcycle Maintenance: An Inquiry Into Values* (1974)

• • •

What do you suppose will satisfy the soul except to walk free and own no superior?
—WALT WHITMAN, "Laws for Creations"

• • •

A mathematical formula for happiness: *Reality* divided by *Expectations*. There were two ways to be happy: improve your reality or lower your expectations.
—JODI PICOULT, *Nineteen Minutes* (2007)

• • •

In the name of God, stop a moment, cease your work,
look around you.
—LEO TOLSTOY

• • •

If you are irritated by every rub,
how will your mirror be polished?
—RUMI

• • •

The most important kind of freedom is to be what you really are.
You trade in your reality for a role. You trade in your sense
for an act. You give up your ability to feel, and in exchange,
put on a mask. There can't be any large-scale revolution until
there's a personal revolution, on an individual level.
It's got to happen inside first.
—JIM MORRISON

• • •

There are no traffic jams on the extra mile.
—Zig Ziglar

● ● ●

Make voyages. Attempt them. There's nothing else.
—Tennessee Williams, *Camino Real* (1953)

● ● ●

It's more fun to think of the future than dwell on the past.
—Sara Shepard, *Unbelievable* (2008)

● ● ●

We are all in the gutter, but some of us are looking at the stars.
—OSCAR WILDE

• • •

Hope is the thing with feathers
That perches in the soul,
And sings the tune—without the words,
And never stops at all.
—EMILY DICKINSON, "Hope is the Thing With Feathers" (1878)

• • •

Weekends don't count unless you spend them doing something
completely pointless.
—BILL WATTERSON

• • •

Real courage is doing the right thing when nobody's looking.
Doing the unpopular thing because it's what you believe, and the
heck with everybody.
—Justin Cronin

• • •

You must learn to take a step back and visualize the whole piece.
If you focus only on the thread given to you, you lose sight of
what it can become.
—Colleen Houck

• • •

Don't let your habits become handcuffs.
—Elizabeth Berg, *The Year of Pleasures* (2005)

• • •

Nothing great was ever achieved without enthusiasm.
—Ralph Waldo Emerson

● ● ●

If you were happy every day of your life, you wouldn't
be a human being. You'd be a game-show host.
—Veronica Sawyer, *Heathers* (1988)

● ● ●

You get what you settle for.
—Louise Sawyer, *Thelma & Louise* (1991)

● ● ●

I'd far rather be happy than right any day.
—SLARTIBARTFAST, *The Hitchhiker's Guide to the Galaxy* (1979)
by Douglas Adams

• • •

I would rather have thirty minutes of wonderful than a lifetime
of nothing special.
—SHELBY, *Steel Magnolias* (1989)

• • •

We deem those happy who, from the experience of life,
have learned to bear its ills, without being overcome by them.
—JUVENAL

• • •

What lies behind us and what lies before us are tiny matters
compared to what lies within us.
—HENRY STANLEY HASKINS

• • •

Knowledge of what is possible is the beginning of happiness.
—GEORGE SANTAYANA

• • •

Cynicism cripples our imagination and limits our ability to see
faint possibilities amidst glaring problems.
—CORY BOOKER

• • •

Life appears to me too short to be spent in nursing animosity
or registering wrongs.
—CHARLOTTE BRONTË, *Jane Eyre* (1847)

• • •

Our great human adventure is the evolution of consciousness.
We are in this life to enlarge the soul, liberate the spirit,
and light up the brain.
—TOM ROBBINS, *Wild Ducks Flying Backward* (2005)

• • •

There is a road from the eye to the heart that does not go
through the intellect.
—G. K. CHESTERTON

• • •

Spend all you have for loveliness,
Buy it and never count the cost;
For one white singing hour of peace
Count many a year of strife well lost,
And for a breath of ecstasy
Give all you have been, or could be.
—SARA TEASDALE, "Barter" (1917)

● ● ●

Hope is not the conviction that something will turn out well,
but the certainty that something makes sense,
regardless of how it turns out.
—VÁCLAV HAVEL

● ● ●

4

Life's Journeys

It is clear the future holds great opportunities. It also holds pitfalls. The trick will be to avoid the pitfalls, seize the opportunities, and get back home by six o'clock.
—WOODY ALLEN, *Side Effects* (1980)

• • •

The real voyage of discovery consists not in seeking new landscapes but in having new eyes.
—MARCEL PROUST

• • •

Believe you can and you're halfway there.
—THEODORE ROOSEVELT

• • •

Do you know that "if" is the middle word in life?
—PHOTOJOURNALIST, *Apocalypse Now* (1979)

● ● ●

Future. That period of time in which our affairs prosper,
our friends are true, and our happiness is assured.
—AMBROSE BIERCE

● ● ●

Do you know, in Sanskrit, the root of the verb
"to be" is the same as "to grow"?
—ANDRE GREGORY, *My Dinner with Andre* (1981)

● ● ●

The life given us, by nature is short; but the memory
of a well-spent life is eternal.
—CICERO

• • •

It is in the knowledge of the genuine conditions of our lives that
we must draw our strength to live and our reasons for living.
—SIMONE DE BEAUVOIR

• • •

The dream was always running ahead of me. To catch up,
to live for a moment in unison, was the miracle.
—ANAÏS NIN

• • •

Any road followed precisely to its end leads precisely nowhere.
—FRANK HERBERT, *Dune* (1965)

• • •

Toto, I've a feeling we're not in Kansas anymore.
—DOROTHY, *The Wizard of Oz* (1939)

• • •

I don't like things that finish.
One must begin something else right away.
—TOM, *Last Tango in Paris* (1972)

• • •

Don't worry about the future. Or worry, but know that worrying is as effective as trying to solve an algebra equation by chewing bubble gum. The real troubles in your life are apt to be things that never crossed your worried mind, the kind that blindside you at 4 p.m. on some idle Tuesday.
—MARY SCHMICH

• • •

Stories never really end . . . even if the books like to pretend they do. Stories always go on. They don't end on the last page, any more than they begin on the first page.
—CORNELIA FUNKE, *Inkspell* (2005)

• • •

Why didn't I learn to treat everything like it was the last time? My greatest regret was how much I believed in the future.
—JONATHAN SAFRAN FOER,
Extremely Loud and Incredibly Close (2005)

• • •

The dictionary is the only place that success comes before work.
Work is the key to success, and hard work can help
you accomplish anything.
—Vince Lombardi

• • •

Guilt starts as a feeling of failure.
—Frank Herbert

• • •

Why choose to fail when success is an option?
—Jillian Michaels

• • •

The day we fret about the future is the day we leave our
childhood behind.
—KVOTHE, *The Name of the Wind* (2007) by Patrick Rothfuss

• • •

All paths are present, always . . .
and we can but choose among them.
—JACQUELINE CAREY, *Kushiel's Chosen* (2002)

• • •

Even if things don't unfold the way you expected,
don't be disheartened or give up.
One who continues to advance will win in the end.
—DAISAKU IKEDA

• • •

Tomorrow is a new day; begin it well and serenely and
with too high a spirit to be encumbered with
your old nonsense.
—RALPH WALDO EMERSON

• • •

All the time you're saying to yourself, "I could do that,
but I won't"–which is just another way of saying
that you can't.
—RICHARD P. FEYNMAN, *Surely You're Joking,
Mr. Feynman!* (1985)

• • •

Know from whence you came. If you know whence you came,
there are absolutely no limitations to where you can go.
—James Baldwin

• • •

Time to toss the dice
—Robert Jordan, *The Wheel of Time*

• • •

Trees that are slow to grow bear the best fruit.
—Molière

• • •

A sailor chooses the wind that takes the ship from a safe port.
Ah, yes, but once you're abroad, as you have seen,
winds have a mind of their own. Be careful, Charlotte,
careful of the wind you choose.
—AVI, *True Confessions of Charlotte Doyle* (1990)

• • •

Some day you will be old enough to start reading
fairy tales again.
—C. S. LEWIS

• • •

You know, some people say life is short and that you could get hit
by a bus at any moment and that you have to live each day like
it's your last. Bullshit. Life is long. You're probably not gonna get
hit by a bus. And you're gonna have to live with the choices you
make for the next fifty years.
—CHRIS ROCK

• • •

Courage doesn't always roar. Sometimes courage is the quiet voice at the end of the day saying, "I will try again tomorrow."
—MARY ANNE RADMACHER

● ● ●

Realize that true happiness lies within you. Waste no time and effort searching for peace and contentment and joy in the world outside. Remember that there is no happiness in having or in getting, but only in giving. Reach out. Share. Smile. Hug. Happiness is a perfume you cannot pour on others without getting a few drops on yourself.
—OG MANDINO

● ● ●

5

Applying What You've Learned

Knowledge itself is power.
—Francis Bacon, *Sacred Meditations* (1597)

• • •

Education is the great engine of personal development.
It is through education that the daughter of a peasant can become
a doctor, that the son of a mineworker can become the head of
the mine, that a child of farmworkers can become the president
of a great nation. It is what we make out of what we have,
not what we are given, that separates one person from another.
—Nelson Mandela, *Long Walk to Freedom* (1994)

• • •

Nurture your minds with great thoughts.
To believe in the heroic makes heroes.
—BENJAMIN DISRAELI

• • •

Let the refining and improving of your own life keep you so busy
that you have little time to criticize others.
—H. JACKSON BROWN, JR.

• • •

Books can truly change our lives: the lives of those who read
them, the lives of those who write them.
Readers and writers alike discover things
they never knew about the world and about themselves.
—LLOYD ALEXANDER, *Time Cat* (1963)

• • •

Be brave enough to live life creatively. The creative place where no one else has ever been.
—ALAN ALDA

• • •

Sit in a room and read—and read and read. And read the right books by the right people. Your mind is brought onto that level, and you have a nice, mild, slow-burning rapture all the time.
—JOSEPH CAMPBELL, *The Power of Myth* (1988)

• • •

There are two ways to reach me: by way of kisses or by way of the imagination. But there is a hierarchy: the kisses alone don't work.
—ANAÏS NIN, *Henry and June* (1986)

• • •

Be creative, be useful, be practical, be generous,
and finish big.
—LISA GENOVA

● ● ●

To know you are ignorant is the beginning of wisdom.
—MARION ZIMMER BRADLEY

● ● ●

Employ your time in improving yourself by other men's writings
so that you shall come easily by what
others have labored hard for.
—SOCRATES

● ● ●

The first duty of a man is to think for himself.
—JOSÉ MARTÍ

● ● ●

If you fail to prepare, you're prepared to fail.
—MARK SPITZ

● ● ●

Invisible things are the only realities.
—EDGAR ALLEN POE, *Loss of Breath* (1832)

● ● ●

Beyond work and love, I would add two other ingredients that
give meaning to life. First, to fulfill whatever talents
we are born with. However blessed we are by fate with different
abilities and strengths, we should try to develop them to the
fullest, rather than allow them to atrophy and decay. We all
know individuals who did not fulfill the promise they showed
in childhood. Many of them became haunted by the image of
what they might have become. Instead of blaming fate, I think
we should accept ourselves as we are and try to fulfill whatever
dreams are within our capability.

Second, we should try to leave the world a better place than
when we entered it. As individuals, we can make a difference,
whether it is to probe the secrets of Nature, to clean up the
environment and work for peace and social justice, or to nurture
the inquisitive, vibrant spirit of the young by being
a mentor and a guide.
—MICHIO KAKU

● ● ●

To me, all creativity is magic. Ideas start out in the empty void of your head—and they end up as a material thing, like a book you can hold in your hand. That is the magical process. It's an alchemical thing. Yes, we do get the gold out of it but that's not the most important thing. It's the work itself.

—ALAN MOORE

• • •

The summit of happiness is reached when a person is ready to be what he is.

—ERASMUS

• • •

Don't only practice your art, but force your way into its secrets, for it and knowledge can raise men to the divine.

—LUDWIG VAN BEETHOVEN

• • •

When choosing the lesser of two evils, always remember,
it is still an evil.
—MAX LERNER

• • •

Never let yourself be persuaded that any one Great Man,
any one leader, is necessary to the salvation of America.
When America consists of one leader and
158 million followers, it will no longer be America.
—DWIGHT D. EISENHOWER

• • •

He stood at the window of the empty cafe and watched the activities in the square and he said that it was good that God kept the truths of life from the young as they were starting out or else they'd have no heart to start at all.
—CORMAC MCCARTHY, *All the Pretty Horses* (1992)

• • •

Accepting oneself does not preclude an attempt to become better.
—FLANNERY O'CONNOR

• • •

People have only as much liberty as they have the intelligence to want and the courage to take.
—EMMA GOLDMAN

• • •

The greatest ideas are the simplest.
—WILLIAM GOLDING, *Lord of the Flies* (1954)

• • •

Spoon feeding in the long run teaches us nothing
but the shape of the spoon.
—E. M. FORSTER

• • •

A man, though wise, should never be ashamed of learning more,
and must unbend his mind.
—SOPHOCLES, *Antigone*

• • •

The essence of the independent mind lies not in what it thinks,
but in how it thinks.

—CHRISTOPHER HITCHENS, *Letters to a Young Contrarian* (2001)

• • •

For me, I am driven by two main philosophies: know more today
about the world than I knew yesterday and lessen the suffering of
others. You'd be surprised how far that gets you.

—NEIL DEGRASSE TYSON

• • •

Adapt what is useful, reject what is useless, and add what is
specifically your own.

—BRUCE LEE

• • •

An idea is salvation by imagination.
—Frank Lloyd Wright

• • •

There is a time in every man's education when he arrives at the conviction that envy is ignorance; that imitation is suicide; that he must take himself for better, for worse, as his portion; that though the wide universe is full of good, no kernel of nourishing corn can come to him but through his toil bestowed on that plot of ground which is given to him to till. The power which resides in him is new in nature, and none but he knows what that is which he can do, nor does he know until he has tried.
—Ralph Waldo Emerson, *Self-Reliance* (1841)

• • •

It is much easier to be brave if you do not know everything.
—Lois Lowry

• • •

Everyone has his own reality in which, if one is not too cautious, timid or frightened, one swims. This is the only reality there is.
—HENRY MILLER, *Stand Still Like the Hummingbird* (1962)

• • •

A goal without a plan is just a wish.
—ANTOINE DE SAINT-EXUPÉRY

• • •

You're never given a dream without also being given
the power to make it true.
—RICHARD BACH, *Illusions: The Adventures of a Reluctant
Messiah* (1977)

• • •

People don't realize how a man's whole life can be changed
by one book.
—MALCOM X, *The Autobiography of Malcolm X* (1965)

• • •

When analytic thought, the knife, is applied to experience,
something is always killed in the process.
—ROBERT M. PIRSIG, *Zen and the Art of Motorcycle Maintenance:
An Inquiry Into Values* (1974)

• • •

Everything you can imagine is real.
—PABLO PICASSO

• • •

I am enough of an artist to draw freely upon my imagination. Imagination is more important than knowledge. Knowledge is limited. Imagination encircles the world.
—ALBERT EINSTEIN

• • •

Everybody has a secret world inside of them. All of the people of the world, I mean everybody. No matter how dull and boring they are on the outside, inside them they've all got unimaginable, magnificent, wonderful, stupid, amazing worlds. Not just one world. Hundreds of them. Thousands maybe.
—NEIL GAIMAN, *The Sandman*

• • •

You can only be afraid of what you think you know.
—Jiddu Krishnamurti

• • •

To accomplish great things, we must not only act but also dream,
not only plan, but also believe!
—Anatole France

• • •

Each man should frame life so that at some future
hour fact and his dreaming meet.
—Victor Hugo

• • •

Daylight is a dream if you live with your eyes closed.
—BARTON FINK, *Barton Fink* (1991)

● ● ●

It's called wisdom. It comes to us suddenly. We realize the
difference between what's real and deep and lasting versus the
superficial payoff of the moment.
—BEN, *Crimes and Misdemeanors* (1989)

● ● ●

So long as we learn, it doesn't matter who teaches us, does it?
—MRS. JOSEPH, *To Sir with Love* (1967)

● ● ●

You are never too old to set another goal
or to dream a new dream.
—C. S. LEWIS

• • •

Graduation is only a concept.
In real life every day you graduate.
Graduation is a process that goes on until
the last day of your life. If you can grasp that,
you'll make a difference.
—ARIE PENCOVICI

• • •

We live less than the time it takes to blink an eye, if we measure
our lives against eternity . . . a blink of an eye in itself is nothing.
But the eye that blinks, that is something. A span of life is
nothing. But the man who lives that span, he is something.
He can fill that tiny span with meaning, so its quality is
immeasurable though its quantity may be insignificant. . . .
A man must fill his life with meaning, meaning is not
automatically given to life.
—REUVEN'S FATHER, *The Chosen* (1967) by Chaim Potok

● ● ●

6

Staring Down Adversity

Never forget what you are,
for surely the world will not.
Make it your strength.
Then it can never be your weakness.
Armor yourself in it,
and it will never be used to hurt you.
—Tyrion Lannister, *A Game of Thrones* (1996)
by George R. R. Martin

• • •

The greatest glory in living lies not in never falling,
but in rising every time we fall.
—Nelson Mandela, *Long Walk to Freedom* (1994)

• • •

The question isn't who is going to let me;
it's who is going to stop me.
—AYN RAND

• • •

Faithless is he that says farewell when the road darkens.
—GIMLI, *The Fellowship of the Ring* (1954) by J. R. R. Tolkien

• • •

Men's best successes come after their disappointments.
—HENRY WARD BEECHER

• • •

If we had no winter, the spring would not be so pleasant:
if we did not sometimes taste of adversity,
prosperity would not be so welcome.
—ANNE BRADSTREET, "Meditations Divine and Moral" (1664)

● ● ●

Even a happy life cannot be without a measure of darkness,
and the word *happy* would lose its meaning if it were not
balanced by sadness. It is far better to take things as they come
along with patience and equanimity.
—CARL JUNG

● ● ●

If you lose your head and you give up, then you neither
live nor win. That's just the way it is.
—JOSEY WALES, *The Outlaw Josey Wales* (1976)

• • •

If you can't fly then run, if you can't run then walk,
if you can't walk then crawl, but whatever you do you have to
keep moving forward.
—MARTIN LUTHER KING, JR.

• • •

Scar tissue is stronger than regular tissue.
Realize the strength, move on.
—HENRY ROLLINS

• • •

Yes, terrible things happen, but sometimes those terrible
things—they save you.
—CHUCK PALAHNIUK, *Haunted* (2005)

• • •

Painful as it may be, a significant emotional event can be the
catalyst for choosing a direction that serves us—and those
around us—more effectively. Look for the learning.
—LOUISA MAY ALCOTT

• • •

If you can talk with crowds and keep your virtue,
Or walk with Kings—nor lose the common touch,
If neither foes nor loving friends can hurt you,
If all men count with you, but none too much;
If you can fill the unforgiving minute
With sixty seconds' worth of distance run,
Yours is the Earth and everything that's in it,
And—which is more—you'll be a Man, my son!
RUDYARD KIPLING, "If—" (1910)

• • •

I never said it would be easy, I only said it would be worth it.
—MAE WEST

• • •

I know that pain is the most important thing in the universes. Greater than survival, greater than love, greater even than the beauty it brings about. For without pain, there can be no pleasure. Without sadness, there can be no happiness. Without misery there can be no beauty. And without these, life is endless, hopeless, doomed and damned.
Adult. You have become adult.
—HARLAN ELLISON, "Paingod" (1965)

• • •

Life is not an easy matter . . . You cannot live through it without falling into frustration and cynicism unless you have before you a great idea which raises you above personal misery, above weakness, above all kinds of perfidy and baseness.
—LEON TROTSKY, *Diary in Exile, 1935*

• • •

The fishermen know that the sea is dangerous and the storm terrible, but they have never found these dangers sufficient reason for remaining ashore.
—VINCENT VAN GOGH

• • •

Who would bring light must endure burning.
—DAVID ZINDELL, *The Wild* (1995)

• • •

Every adversity, every failure, every heartache carries
with it the seed of an equal or greater benefit.
—NAPOLEON HILL

• • •

Mistakes are the portals of discovery.
—CECELIA AHERN

• • •

Say to yourself in the early morning: I shall meet today inquisitive, ungrateful, violent, treacherous, envious, uncharitable men. All these things have come upon them through ignorance of real good and ill.
—MARCUS AURELIUS, *Meditations*

• • •

Ruin is a gift. Ruin is the road to transformation.
—ELIZABETH GILBERT, *Eat, Pray, Love* (2006)

• • •

I must say a word about fear. It is life's only true opponent. Only fear can defeat life.
—YANN MARTEL, *Life of Pi* (2001)

• • •

Sometimes you just have to bite your upper lip and put
sunglasses on.
—BOB DYLAN, *Chronicles: Volume One* (2004)

• • •

Sometimes you just have to put on lip gloss
and pretend to be psyched.
—MINDY KALING

• • •

Ever tried. Ever failed. No matter. Try again.
Fail again. Fail better.
—SAMUEL BECKETT, *Worstward Ho* (1983)

• • •

Real courage is when you know you're licked before you begin,
but you begin anyway and see it through no matter what.
—HARPER LEE, *To Kill a Mockingbird* (1960)

• • •

Storms make trees take deeper roots.
—DOLLY PARTON

• • •

I love the man that can smile in trouble, that can gather strength
from distress, and grow brave by reflection.
'Tis the business of little minds to shrink; but he whose heart is
firm, and whose conscience approves his conduct,
will pursue his principles unto death.
—THOMAS PAINE, *The American Crisis*

• • •

In the forest, there was a crooked tree and a straight tree. Every
day, the straight tree would say to the crooked tree, "Look at
me . . . I'm tall, and I'm straight, and I'm handsome. Look at
you . . . you're all crooked and bent over. No one wants to look at
you." And they grew up in that forest together. And then one day
the loggers came, and they saw the crooked tree and the straight
tree, and they said, "Just cut the straight trees and leave the
rest." So the loggers turned all the straight trees into lumber and
toothpicks and paper. And the crooked tree is still there, growing
stronger and stranger every day.
—TOM WAITS

• • •

Tough times never last. Tough people do
—ROBERT H. SCHULLER

• • •

Show me a guy who's afraid to look bad, and I'll show you a guy
you can beat every time.
—LOU BROCK

• • •

Never let your head hang down. Never give up and sit down and
grieve. Find another way.
—SATCHEL PAIGE

• • •

LISTAGEM 11-2

ção de dados e aos

using System.Collections

protected void Page_Load(obje

(!this.IsPostBack)

.TechnologyDe

nologyDes

XI.D

hO);

logyName';

echList;

"TechnologyName";

urce = techList;

-Field = "TechnologyName";

4List;

hnologyName";

Adversity introduces a man to himself.
—ALBERT EINSTEIN

• • •

Until you have suffered much in your heart,
you cannot learn humility.
—ELDER THADDEUS OF VITOVNICA

• • •

Oh yes, the past can hurt. But the from way I see it,
you can either run from it, or learn from it.
—RAFIKI, *The Lion King* (1994)

• • •

You can't be brave if you've only had wonderful
things happen to you.
—MARY TYLER MOORE

• • •

It's not whether you get knocked down; it's whether you get up.
—VINCE LOMBARDI

• • •

So you must not be frightened if a sadness rises up before you larger than any you have ever seen; if a restiveness, like light and cloud shadows, passes over your hands and over all you do. You must think that something is happening with you, that life has not forgotten you, that it holds you in its hand; it will not let you fall. Why do you want to shut out of your life any uneasiness, any miseries, or any depressions? For after all, you do not know what work these conditions are doing inside you.

—RAINER MARIA RILKE, to Franz Xaver Kappus

• • •

7

How to Live Your Life

Be undeniably good.
—STEVE MARTIN

• • •

Seek always to do some good, somewhere . . . Even if it's a little
thing, so something for those that need help, something for
which you get no pay but the privilege of doing it
—ALBERT SCHWEITZER

• • •

There are heroisms all round us waiting to be done.
—SIR ARTHUR CONAN DOYLE

• • •

The consequences of every act are included in the act itself.
—GEORGE ORWELL, *Nineteen Eighty-Four* (1949)

• • •

Each of our acts makes a statement as to our purpose.
—LEO BUSCAGLIA

• • •

Doing nothing for others is the undoing of ourselves.
—HORACE MANN

• • •

A concept is a brick. It can be used to build a courthouse of reason. Or it can be thrown through the window.
—GILLES DELEUZE

• • •

We have been called to heal wounds, to unite what has fallen apart, and to bring home those who have lost their way.
—ST. FRANCIS OF ASSISSI

• • •

You're not a human being until you value something more than
the life of your body. And the greater the thing you live
and die for the greater you are.
—ORSON SCOTT CARD, *The Worthing Chronicle* (1983)

● ● ●

Nothing great will ever be achieved without great men,
and men are great only if they are determined to be so.
—CHARLES DE GAULLE

● ● ●

Caution and conservatism are expected of old age; but when the
young men of a nation are possessed of such a spirit,
when they are afraid of the noise and strife caused by the new
applications of the truth, Heaven save the land!
Its funeral bell has already rung.
—HENRY WARD BEECHER,
Prayers from the Plymouth Pulpit (1867)

● ● ●

You may choose to look the other way but you can never say
again that you did not know.
—WILLIAM WILBERFORCE

• • •

Whatsoever a man soweth, that shall he also reap.
—GALATIANS 6:7

• • •

The problems of the world cannot possibly be solved by skeptics
or cynics whose horizons are limited by the obvious realities.
We need men who can dream of things that never were.
—JOHN KEATS

• • •

If you do something too good, then, after a while,
if you don't watch it, you start showing off.
And then you're not as good any more.
—HOLDEN CAULFIELD, *The Catcher in the Rye* (1951)
by J. D. Salinger

• • •

If you can't you must, and if you must you can.
—TONY ROBBINS

• • •

The depth and strength of a human character are defined by its
moral reserves. People reveal themselves completely only when
they are thrown out of the customary conditions of their life,
for only then do they have to fall back on their reserves.
—LEON TROTSKY, *Diary in Exile, 1935*

• • •

God never gives us discernment in order that we may criticize,
but that we may intercede.
—Oswald Chambers

• • •

Thou shalt not be a victim, thou shalt not be a perpetrator,
but, above all, thou shalt not be a bystander.
—Yehuda Bauer

• • •

I think of few heroic actions, which cannot be traced to the artistical impulse. He who does great deeds, does them from his innate sensitiveness to moral beauty.
—WALT WHITMAN

• • •

If you think you are too small to make a difference,
try sleeping with a mosquito.
—DALAI LAMA XIV

• • •

Change will not come if we wait for some other person, or if we wait for some other time. We are the ones we've been waiting for. We are the change that we seek.
—BARACK OBAMA

• • •

What I stand for is what I stand on.
—Wendell Berry

• • •

What affects one in a major way, affects all in a minor way.
—Martin Luther King, Jr.

• • •

Doing nothing for others is the undoing of ourselves.
—Horace Mann

• • •

Never doubt that a small group of thoughtful,
committed, citizens can change the world. Indeed,
it is the only thing that ever has.
—Margaret Mead

• • •

Do what you can, with what you have, where you are.
—Theodore Roosevelt

• • •

Never be bullied into silence.
Never allow yourself to be made a victim. Accept no one's
definition of your life, but define yourself.
—Harvey Fierstein

• • •

The will is everything. If you make yourself more than just a man, if you devote yourself to an ideal, you become something else entirely. Are you ready to begin?
—HENRI DUCARD, *Batman Begins* (2005)

• • •

With great power comes great responsibility.
—UNCLE BEN, *Amazing Fantasy #15* (1962)
by Stan Lee and Steve Ditko

• • •

What we achieve inwardly will change outer reality.
—PLUTARCH

• • •

This world demands the qualities of youth; not a time of life but
a state of mind, a temper of the will, a quality of the imagination,
a predominance of courage over timidity, of the appetite for
adventure over the life of ease.
—ROBERT F. KENNEDY

• • •

To live fully, we must learn to use things and love people,
and not love things and use people.
—JOHN POWELL

• • •

8

The Meaning of Success

It is not enough to be industrious; so are the ants.
What are you industrious about?
—HENRY DAVID THOREAU, to Harrison Blake

• • •

Anything can be great. I don't care, bricklaying can be great
if a guy knows what he's doing and why
and if he can make it come off.
—FAST EDDIE FELSON, *The Hustler* (1961)

• • •

It is never too late to be what you might have been.
—GEORGE ELIOT

• • •

The best revenge is massive success.
—FRANK SINATRA

• • •

We are what we pretend to be, so we must be careful
what we pretend to be.
—KURT VONNEGUT

• • •

Nothing of character is really permanent
but virtue and personal worth.
—DANIEL WEBSTER

• • •

It's a lie to think you're not good enough. It's a lie to think you're not worth anything.
—Nick Vujicic

• • •

No other success can compensate for failure in the home.
—J. E. McCullough

• • •

Character and personal force are the only investments that are worth anything.
—WALT WHITMAN

• • •

Try not to become a man of success but a man of value.
—ALBERT EINSTEIN

• • •

It's not who you are underneath, it's what you do that defines you.
—RACHEL DAWES, *Batman Begins* (2005)

• • •

I'd rather be a rising ape than a falling angel.
—TERRY PRATCHETT

• • •

The worst part of success is trying to find someone
who is happy for you.
—BETTE MIDLER

• • •

I'd rather be hated for who I am, than loved for who I am not.
—KURT COBAIN

• • •

Happiness depends more on the inward disposition of mind than on outward circumstances.
—BENJAMIN FRANKLIN

• • •

There's nothing wrong with you. There's a lot wrong with the world you live in. And definitely get out of high school and make everyone sorry.
—CHRIS COLFER

• • •

When I was growing up I always wanted to be someone.
Now I realize I should have been more specific.
—LILY TOMLIN

• • •

All is ephemeral—fame and the famous as well.
—MARCUS AURELIUS, *Meditations*

• • •

We are all worms, but I do believe that I am a glow worm.
—WINSTON CHURCHILL

• • •

Write it, shoot it, publish it, crochet it, sauté it, whatever. *Make.*
—JOSS WHEDON

• • •

Your success story is a bigger story than whatever
you're trying to say on stage. . . . Success makes life easier.
It doesn't make living easier.
—BRUCE SPRINGSTEEN

• • •

If people reach perfection they vanish, you know.
—T. H. WHITE, *The Once and Future King* (1958)

• • •

I attribute my success to this—I never gave or took any excuse.
—FLORENCE NIGHTINGALE

• • •

Well, it's no trick to make a lot of money . . . if all you want to do
is make a lot of money.
—BERNSTEIN, *Citizen Kane* (1941)

• • •

Forget yourself and go to work.
—Bryant S. Hinckley

● ● ●

Come friends, it's not too late to seek a newer world.
—Alfred Tennyson

● ● ●

9

Commencement Wisdom

In the day-to-day trenches of adult life, there is actually no such
thing as atheism. There is no such thing as not worshipping.
Everybody worships. The only choice we get is what to worship.
—DAVID FOSTER WALLACE, Kenyon College (2005)

• • •

Young people who pretend to be wise to the ways of the world
are mostly just cynics. Cynicism masquerades as wisdom, but it
is the farthest thing from it. Because cynics don't learn anything.
Because cynicism is a self-imposed blindness, a rejection of
the world because we are afraid it will hurt us or disappoint us.
Cynics always say no. But saying yes begins things. Saying yes is
how things grow. Saying yes leads to knowledge. Yes is for young
people. So for as long as you have the strength to, say yes.
—STEPHEN COLBERT, Knox College (2006)

• • •

Your time is limited, so don't waste it living someone else's life.
Don't be trapped by dogma—which is living with the results of
other people's thinking. Don't let the noise of others' opinions
drown out your own inner voice. And most important, have the
courage to follow your heart and intuition.
They somehow already know what you truly want to become.
Everything else is secondary.
—STEVE JOBS, Stanford University (2005)

• • •

I've had a lot of success. I've had a lot of failure. I've looked good.
I've looked bad. I've been praised. And I've been criticized.
But my mistakes have been necessary. I've dwelled on my failures
today because, as graduates of Harvard, your biggest liability
is your need to succeed, your need to always find yourself on
the sweet side of the bell curve. Success is a lot like a bright
white tuxedo. You feel terrific when you get it, but then you're
desperately afraid of getting it dirty, of spoiling it.
—CONAN O'BRIEN, Harvard University (2000)

• • •

So when you get out there in the world, ladies and gentlemen, you're going to find yourself surrounded by shouting, red-in-the-face, stomping-mad politicians, radio yakmeisters and, yes, sad to say, newspaper columnists, telling you "you never had it so bad" and otherwise trying to spoil your day. When they come at you with that, ladies and gentlemen, give them a wink and a smile and a good view of your departing back. And as you stroll away, bend down to smell a flower.
—RUSSELL BAKER, Connecticut College (1995)

• • •

Never give in, never give in, never, never, never—in nothing, great or small, large or petty—never give in except to convictions of great honor and good sense.
—WINSTON CHURCHILL, Harrow School (1941)

• • •

The really important kind of freedom involves attention and awareness and discipline, and being able truly to care about other people and to sacrifice for them over and over in myriad petty, unsexy ways every day. That is real freedom. That is being educated, and understanding how to think. The alternative is unconsciousness, the default setting, the rat race, the constant gnawing sense of having had, and lost, some infinite thing.
—DAVID FOSTER WALLACE, Kenyon College (2005)

• • •

I was not exceptional here, and am not now. I was mediocre here. And I'm not saying aim low. Not everybody can wander around in an alcoholic haze and then at forty just, you know, decide to be president. You've got to really work hard to try to . . . I was actually referring to my father.
—JON STEWART, William & Mary College (2004)

• • •

I hope you work hard to preserve the friendships you've made here, to savor their general and universal warmth, their soul purifying practices, the unique entity that each friendship represents, the bond that grows for no reason that you could ever understand beforehand, but only because you were you and she was she.
—DAVID BROOKS, Skidmore College (2013)

• • •

Success may not come quickly or easily. But if you strive to do what's right, if you work harder and dream bigger, if you set an example in your own lives and do your part to help meet the challenges of our time, then I'm confident that, together, we will continue the never-ending task of perfecting our union.
—BARACK OBAMA, Morehouse College (2013)

• • •

The American Dream has no shortcuts—and no end point. It's is the freedom you have to chart your own journey—and through hard work, to find professional success and personal fulfillment.
—MICHAEL BLOOMBERG, Stanford University (2013)

• • •

And now go, and make interesting mistakes, make amazing mistakes, make glorious and fantastic mistakes. Break rules. Leave the world more interesting for your being here.
Make good art.
—NEIL GAIMAN, University of the Arts (2012)

• • •

You will leave here with a degree, but it does not confirm maturity or judgment. Most of all remember this: You cannot get through this world alone. You need each other. We need you to celebrate one another in a common cause of restoring economic justice and true value, advancing racial and religious tolerance, creating a healthier planet, and most of all, hoping that at some time in our life we can achieve world peace.
—Tom Brokaw, University of Montana (2011)

• • •

Success is not like rain that falls from the sky equally upon everyone. Success is what you reap when you sow with passion and optimism.
—Professor Ahmed Zewail,
California Institute of Technology (2011)

• • •

You graduates are coming of age in an amazing time. As you leave Harvard, you have technology that members of my class never had. You have awareness of global inequity, which we did not have. And with that awareness, you likely also have an informed conscience that will torment you if you abandon these people whose lives you could change with very little effort.
—BILL GATES, Harvard University (2007)

• • •

Rehearsal's over. You're going out there now, you're going to do this thing. How you live matters. You're going to fall down, but the world doesn't care how many times you fall down, as long as it's one fewer than the number of times you get back up.
—AARON SORKIN, Syracuse University (2012)

• • •

All you want to get at the getting place, from the Maserati you may dream about to the retirement fund some broker will try to sell you on, none of that is real. All that lasts is what you pass on. The rest is smoke and mirrors.
—STEPHEN KING, University of Maine (2001)

• • •

I cannot stress enough that the answer to life's questions is often in people's faces. Try putting your iPhones down once in a while, and look in people's faces. People's faces will tell you amazing things. Like if they are angry, or nauseous, or asleep.
—AMY POEHLER, Harvard University (2011)

• • •

It is impossible to live without failing at something, unless you live so cautiously that you might as well not have lived at all—in which case, you fail by default.
—J. K. ROWLING, Harvard University (2008)

• • •

We have to continue to shake off what we sometimes think we know in order to lend our imaginations to vibrant and sometimes agonistic spectrums of experience.
—JUDITH BUTLER, McGill University (2013)

• • •

Cleverness is a gift, kindness is a choice. Gifts are easy—they're given after all. Choices can be hard. You can seduce yourself with your gifts if you're not careful, and if you do, it'll probably be to the detriment of your choices.
—JEFF BEZOS, Princeton University (2010)

• • •

Integrate what you believe into every single area of your life. Take your heart to work, and ask the most and best of everybody else too. Don't let your special character and values—the secret that you know and no one else does, the truth—don't let that get swallowed up by the great chewing complacency.
—MERYL STREEP, Vassar College (1983)

• • •

My commandment is: "Thou shalt not stand idly by," which means that where you see an injustice, do not stand idly by. Where you hear of a person or a group being persecuted, do not stand idly by. Where there is something wrong with the community around you—or far away—do not stand idly by. You must intervene; you must interfere.
—ELIE WIESEL, Washington University in St. Louis (2011)

• • •

In a vital community, as in one's life,
education ought not to stand still.
—DAVID McCULLOUGH,
University of Massachusetts in Boston (1998)

• • •

The Armenians have a saying, that in the hour of your birth, God thumbprints thee with a genetic thumbprint in the middle of your forehead. But in the hour of your birth, that thumbprint vanishes back into your flesh. Your job, as young people, is to look in the mirror every day of your life, and see the shape of that genetic thumbprint. And find out just who in the hell you are. It's a big job, but a wonderful job.
—RAY BRADBURY, California Institute of Technology (2000)

• • •

You have, which is a rare thing, that ability and the responsibility to listen to the dissent in yourself, to at least give it the floor, because it is the key—not only to consciousness-but to real growth. To accept duality is to earn identity. And identity is something that you are constantly earning. It is not just who you are. It is a process that you must be active in. It's not just parroting your parents or the thoughts of your learned teachers. It is now more than ever about understanding yourself so you can become yourself.
—Joss WHEDON, Wesleyan University (2009)

• • •

If you ever feel that you're at a loss of what to do, get still—very still—and the answer will reach to you ultimately.
—OPRAH WINFREY, Stanford University (2008)

• • •

10

Life, the Universe, and Everything

Do or do not. There is no try.
—Yoda, *Star Wars Episode V: The Empire Strikes Back* (1980)

• • •

Not all those who wander are lost.
—J. R. R. Tolkien, *The Fellowship of the Ring* (1954)

• • •

Life isn't about finding yourself. Life is about creating yourself.
—George Bernard Shaw

• • •

True terror is to wake up one morning and discover that your high school class is running the country.
—KURT VONNEGUT

• • •

When I let go of what I am, I become what I might be.
—LAO TZU

• • •

Sometimes the road less traveled is less traveled for a reason.
—JERRY SEINFELD

• • •

A daydreamer is prepared for most things.
—Joyce Carol Oates

• • •

If you don't have time to do it right,
when will you have the time to do it over?
—John Wooden

• • •

In the end, everything is a gag.
—Charlie Chaplin

• • •

We're in such a hurry most of the time we never get much chance to talk. The result is a kind of endless day-to-day shallowness, a monotony that leaves a person wondering years later where all the time went and sorry that it's all gone.
—ROBERT M. PIRSIG, *Zen and the Art of Motorcycle Maintenance: An Inquiry Into Values* (1974)

• • •

Bones mend. Regret stays with you forever.
—KVOTHE, *The Name of the Wind* (2007) by Patrick Rothfuss

• • •

I am always saying "Glad to've met you" to somebody I'm not at all glad I met. If you want to stay alive, you have to say that stuff, though.
—HOLDEN CAULFIELD, *The Catcher in the Rye* (1951) by J. D. Salinger

• • •

Ah, but a man's reach should exceed his grasp,
Or what's a heaven for?
—ROBERT BROWNING, "Andrea del Sarto" (1855)

• • •

Be not afraid of life. Believe that life is worth living, and your
belief will help create the fact.
—WILLIAM JAMES, "The Will to Believe" (1896)

• • •

When in danger or in doubt, run in circles, scream and shout.
—HERMAN WOUK

• • •

In real life, I assure you, there is no such thing as algebra.
—FRAN LEBOWITZ

• • •

If a black cat crosses your path, it signifies that the animal is
going somewhere.
—GROUCHO MARX

• • •

Weaseling out of things is important to learn. It's what separates
us from the animals. Except the weasel.
—HOMER SIMPSON, *The Simpsons* (1993)

• • •

When in doubt, look intelligent.
—GARRISON KEILLOR

● ● ●

If at first you don't succeed then skydiving definitely isn't for you.
—STEVEN WRIGHT

● ● ●

Just keep going. Everybody gets better if they keep at it.
—TED WILLIAMS

● ● ●

Life is ours to be spent, not to be saved.
—D. H. LAWRENCE

• • •

A sail boat that sails backwards can never see the sun rise.
—BILL COSBY

• • •

This above all: to thine own self be true.
—POLONIUS, *Hamlet* by William Shakespeare

• • •

Life's under no obligation to give us what we expect.
—MARGARET MITCHELL

• • •

There's an old joke: two elderly women are at a Catskill mountain resort, and one of 'em says, "Boy, the food at this place is really terrible." The other one says, "Yeah, I know; and such small portions." Well, that's essentially how I feel about life—full of loneliness, and misery, and suffering, and unhappiness, and it's all over much too quickly
—ALVY SINGER, *Annie Hall* (1977)

• • •

Stop and consider! Life is but a day:
A fragile dewdrop on its perilous way
From a tree's summit
—JOHN KEATS, "Sleep and Poetry"

• • •

Life is problems. Living is solving problems.
—RAYMOND E. FEIST, *Silverthorn* (1986)

● ● ●

Just keep swimming. Just keep swimming. Just keep swimming, swimming, swimming. What do we do? We swim, swim.
—DORY, *Finding Nemo* (2003)

● ● ●

All that happens means something;
nothing you do is ever insignificant.
—ALDOUS HUXLEY, *Crome Yellow* (1921)

● ● ●

Life is like a novel. It's filled with suspense. You have no idea what
is going to happen until you turn the page.
—SIDNEY SHELDON

● ● ●

My formula for life is very simple: in the morning, wake up;
at night, go to sleep. In between I try and occupy myself
as best I can.
—CARY GRANT

● ● ●

I never approve, or disapprove, of anything now.
It is an absurd attitude to take towards life.
—OSCAR WILDE

● ● ●

Nothing is ever enough when what you are looking for isn't what you really want.
—ARIANNA HUFFINGTON

• • •

Ah, ladies and gentlemen, a man lives a sad life when he cannot take anything or anyone seriously.
—MILAN KUNDERA, *Laughable Loves* (1969)

• • •

My point is, life is about balance. The good and the bad. The highs and the lows. The pina and the colada.
—ELLEN DEGENERES

• • •

Index

Index

Index

Index

West, Mae, 128
Whedon, Joss, 61, 171, 193
White, T. H., 171
Whitman, Walt, 64, 154, 165
Wiesel, Elie, 190
Wilberforce, William, 150
Wilde, Oscar, 68, 206
Willard, Francis E., 18
Williams, Ted, 202
Winchell, Walter, 49
Winfrey, Oprah, 193
Winnie-the-Pooh, 29
Wizard of Oz, The, 82
Worstward Ho, 134
Worthing Chronicle, The, 149

Wouk, Herman, 200
Wright, Frank Lloyd, 110
Wright, Steven, 202

X

X, Malcom, 115
xkcd, 16

Z

Zen and the Art of Motorcycle Maintenance: An Inquiry Into Values, 64, 115, 199
Zewail, Ahmed, 183
Zorba the Greek, 29